To all
the imagery
waiting
to be
awakened

Introduction

This book contains original stories and higher order thinking (HOT) questions written specifically for the *Visualizing and Verbalizing Language Comprehension and Thinking*® (V/V®) program.

High in imagery—often focusing on the imagery of color, size, and movement—the paragraphs are self-contained and assist individuals in developing an imaged gestalt. The stories are followed by detail, main idea, conclusion, inference, and prediction questions.

The stories are approximately graded from kindergarten through eighth grade, with several short paragraphs at every level and some multiple paragraphs at most levels. The quantity of the content is identified at the far right margin of each selection. Remember, the Sentence by Sentence step of V/V should have no more than five parts (sentences) to visualize and verbalize. Thus, stories with six or more sentences may be used for the Multiple Sentence and Whole Paragraph steps, or sentences can be combined down to five sentences for the Sentence by Sentence step. Multiple paragraphs may be used for the Paragraph by Paragraph step. Though the stories are graded, *they are not meant to be used to pace individuals through the development of gestalt imagery*. Some individuals will only need to do a few low level paragraphs, while others may need to do more than is provided in this book! Here is some pacing advice.

- Most individuals, unless very young or severely impaired in language processing, should start at Level 3 (third grade). This allows them to begin the V/V process of developing an imaged gestalt without having to cope with complex vocabulary or content.

- You are the diagnostician in deciding when to move from one V/V step to another or from one grade level to another. Here's a tip. Notice how many questions you are having to ask to stimulate imagery. When you notice that images are being generated without the need for much questioning, it's time to move on. In general, note when you are talking less and the student is talking more!

These books have been written specifically for the V/V program to develop comprehension and critical thinking through dual coding. As the eminent cognitive psychologist Allan Paivio said in describing his Dual Coding Theory (DCT), "Cognition is proportional to the extent that the coding mechanisms of mental representations (imagery) and language are integrated." These V/V stories and higher order thinking (HOT) questions are a tool to integrate visualizing and verbalizing—the dual coding of imagery and language—necessary for cognition.

Aristotle said, "Man cannot think without mental imagery." Since without thinking and reasoning we are lost, it is my hope that these V/V stories and HOT questions will assist individuals to reason and communicate better.

Nanci Bell

Visualizing and Verbalizing®

Stories

Nanci Bell

BOOK **2**

LEVEL K-8

Thank you to Val Jones, Jane Miller, and Alison Bell for writing
and editing with me. Who knew it would be so hard to
write stories and HOT questions that fit the V/V program!
Thanks for your patience.

Ivan illustrations by Henry Santos

Remember:

- Start your questions with "What are you picturing for...?"

- Question with choice and contrast. "Did you see the girl big or little?"

- Encourage student(s) to *gesture* and *talk*.

  - Respond to the response. "If you pictured...let's see if that matches the sentence imagery."

    - You can combine sentences to whittle a story down to five sentences for the Sentence by Sentence step.

  - Help student(s) visualize new vocabulary.

  - It is okay to reread a sentence. Use the phrase, "See if you want to add or change anything."

    - Do some stories receptively (student listens) and some expressively (student reads aloud or to self).

  - Question to the gestalt.

Table of Contents

I don't mind eels

   Except as meals

      And the way they feels.

         -Ogden Nash

Primary Level

Primary Level

1.
three sentences

The boys had a red ball. It was fun to kick. Then they hit it with a bat. Pop!

    1. What color did you picture the ball?
    2. What do you think "pop" meant happened in the story?
    3. Why do you think the ball popped?
    4. How do you picture the boys felt when the ball popped?
    5. What do you picture might happen next?

2.
three sentences

Little Jan got a little dog. It was black and white. She named him Spot.

    1. What size did you picture Spot?
    2. Why do you think Jan may have named her dog Spot?
    3. Why do you think Jan may have been given a little dog?
    4. Does Spot's name help you picture him? How?
    5. What is a good title for all the imagery in this story?

3.

The big dog plays in the snow. He makes deep tracks. His thick fur keeps him warm. His name is Snowball.

1. What did you picture for the size of the dog?
2. Why do you think Snowball makes deep tracks in the snow?
3. Do you think Snowball would make deep tracks on a city street? Why?
4. What color did you picture Snowball? Why?
5. What problem would Snowball have if he lost all his fur?

4.

Dan put water on his yellow wagon. He scrubbed the red wheels. He put the wagon in the house. Then his mother came into the room. She put her hand to her mouth.

1. What color did you picture Dan's wagon?
2. Why do you think Dan put his wagon in the house?
3. Why do you think his mother put her hand to her mouth?
4. What do you picture might happen next?
5. What is the main idea of all these images?

Primary Level

5.

four sentences

Tim is a cowboy. He rides a black horse to do his work. He has brown boots. He has a big white cowboy hat.

1. What color did you picture Tim's hat?
2. What kind of jobs do you picture Tim doing when he works?
3. Why do you think Tim rides a horse to do his work instead of driving a car or sitting at a desk?
4. What problem would Tim have if his horse got sick? How might he fix it?
5. What is the main idea of all this imagery?

6.

four sentences

The white puppies dashed across the grass. They dug in the garden. They rolled in the dirt. Then they ran for the open door to the house.

1. What color did you picture the puppies at the beginning of the story?
2. Did you picture the puppies a different color at the end of the story? Why?
3. How do you think the people in the house might have felt when they saw the puppies running in the door?
4. What can you picture happening next?
5. How might the people in the house fix the problem the puppies caused?

7.

The clown sat on a big red ball. Then he rolled off. His big feet flew up in the air. The children laughed.

    1. What did you visualize the clown's feet doing when he fell off the ball?
    2. Why do you think the clown fell off the ball?
    3. Why do you think his feet flew up in the air?
    4. Why did the children laugh?
    5. What can you picture happening next?

8.

Jill liked her new book. She took it with her to the dinner table. She took it to bed at night. Then one day she took it in the bathtub!

    1. Where did you picture Jill taking her book first?
    2. What did you picture might happen to the book at the dinner table?
    3. What do you think might have happened to Jill's book in the bathtub?
    4. Do you think Jill will take her books to the bathtub again? Why or why not?
    5. What is a good title for all these images?

Primary Level

9. five sentences

Kip looked down the dark street. He saw something move. He got ready to run. Then he heard a playful bark. Kip smiled and called out, "Hey Sam, come here."

    1. Where did you picture Kip?
    2. Why do you think Kip got ready to run?
    3. Do you think the dog that barked was Kip's dog? Why?
    4. What might you picture happening next?
    5. Give this a good title.

10. five sentences

A blue bird was in a tree. Then she flew to her nest. There was a lot of chirping. She dropped a worm into the nest. The chirping stopped.

    1. Where did you picture the blue bird sitting?
    2. Why do you think the bird flew down to her nest?
    3. What did you picture chirping?
    4. Why do you think the bird dropped a worm into her nest?
    5. Why do you think the chirping stopped?

11.

The little yellow fish swam slowly in the water. Then he darted into a small cave. A big red fish swam by the cave. Soon the little fish swam out.

    1. What color did you picture the big fish?
    2. Why do you think the little fish darted into the small cave?
    3. How do you think the little fish felt went he saw the big fish?
    4. What might the little fish do if the big fish comes back?
    5. What is the main idea of all these images?

12.

Tom found a big black bug. He put it in a jar and skipped with it to his house. His older sister made a face at the bug in the jar. Tom smiled and opened the lid. His sister screamed and ran away.

    1. How did you picture Tom going to his house—skipping or running?
    2. Why did Tom's sister make a face?
    3. Why do you think Tom smiled when he opened the jar?
    4. Why do you think his sister ran away?
    5. What problem can you picture Tom having if the big black bug jumped out of the jar when he opened the lid?

The cow is of the bovine ilk;
One end is moo, the other, milk.

-Ogden Nash

Level One

Level One

1.
rightfour sentences

The owl hunts at night. It can see very well in the dark. The owl is quiet when it flies. The mice had better hide.

    1. What did it look like in your imagery when the owl was hunting?
    2. Why do you think the owl hunts at night rather than in the day?
    3. Why do you think it is important for the owl to be quiet when it flies?
    4. Why do you think the mice need to hide?
    5. Why do you think we don't see owls very often in the daytime?

2.
rightfour sentences

The red bird sat in a tall tree. She spotted something moving in the green grass. She flew down and pulled a big worm out of the ground. Then she flew to her hungry babies.

    1. What color did you picture the bird?
    2. Do you think the bird had good eyes? Explain.
    3. Why do you think the bird got the worm?
    4. What can you picture happening next?
    5. What is the main idea?

3.

Kate sat in the back seat on the trip. She had toys and books. She had a bottle of water to drink. As soon as they got to Grandma's house, Kate jumped out. She ran to the old house with a smile on her face.

1. Where did you picture Kate sitting in the car?
2. Do you think they were on a long drive or a short one? Why?
3. Why do you think Kate had a smile on her face?
4. What might you picture happening if Grandma wasn't home?
5. What is the main idea of all this imagery?

4.

When the rain stopped, Kim ran outside to play. She jumped in the wet grass. She shook raindrops off the tree branches. She splashed in puddles and got soaked. She finally ran to the house, shivering.

1. What did you picture Kim doing in the puddles?
2. Why do you think she waited until the rain stopped before she went outside?
3. What seems funny about Kim waiting for the rain to stop before she went outside?
4. Why do you think Kim ran back to the house?
5. What can you picture happening next?

Level One

5.

Most baby birds are born with no feathers. As the birds grow up, they grow more and more feathers. Feathers help a bird keep dry in the rain. The feathers also help the bird stay warm in cold weather. When feathers fall out, birds use them in their nests.

1. What did you picture for the baby birds?
2. What can you picture happening if the babies didn't ever grow feathers?
3. How do you think a mother bird might help baby birds in cold weather?
4. Why might feathers be good in nests?
5. What is a good title for all this imagery?

6.

Hail is frozen raindrops. It falls from the sky on cold rainy days. Once in a while hail gets as big as golf balls. Big hail can break windows and dent cars. Many people stay indoors when hail gets big.

1. What kind of weather did you picture when it hails?
2. Why do you think it needs to be cold in order to make hail?
3. Why do you think people stay indoors when hail gets big?
4. What could hail hurt besides people and cars?
5. What is the main idea of all this imagery?

7.

Giraffes are the tallest animals. They are yellow and brown. They can reach very far. They eat leaves from tall trees. A giraffe has to do the splits with its front legs so it can drink from a stream or pond.

    1. What do you picture giraffes eating?
    2. Why do you think giraffes eat leaves and not grass?
    3. Why do you think giraffes have to do the splits to drink?
    4. How might being able to reach higher than other animals be good for giraffes?
    5. What might happen to a giraffe if it lived in a place without trees?

8.

Old Jed was an old yellow cat. He thought he saw a little green bird in a tree. He climbed up the tree. Then, poof, the leaf blew away. Old Jed let out a sad meow.

    1. What color did you picture Old Jed?
    2. Why did Old Jed climb up the tree?
    3. Do you think there was really a green bird in the tree?
    4. Why did Old Jed think the green leaf was a green bird?
    5. How do you think Old Jed felt when the leaf blew away?

Level One

9.

six sentences

Fred had a warty green toad he kept in his room. Toady lived in an old fish tank filled with rocks and leaves. One day, Fred picked up Toady but Toady quickly jumped on Fred's bed. Then he jumped to the floor. Fred looked all day for his toad. That night as he went to sleep he could hear, "Ribbit, ribbit."

1. What did you picture for Toady?
2. Why do you think Toady jumped from Fred's hand but never jumped out of his tank?
3. Do you think Toady got out of Fred's room that day? Why?
4. What can you picture might happen next?
5. What problems might Fred and Toady have if Fred doesn't find his toad?

10.

seven sentences

Snow floated down all night outside Jill's window. Her yard was covered with a very thick blanket of white. Jill woke up and heard something roar. She jumped out of bed and looked out the window. She gasped at all the snow she saw. She could still hear the roaring sound. Then she saw the big snowplow making its way on the road.

1. What was making the roaring sound?
2. Why do you think Jill woke up?
3. Why do you think Jill jumped out of bed?
4. How do you think Jill felt when looked out the window? Why?
5. Why do you think it might be important for the snowplow to come?

11.

The inchworm has a long, thin body. But it only has legs at its front and back ends. This gives it a very funny walk.

First, the back legs walk. Then its body goes up in the middle. Last, the front legs walk and the body goes down. Each time it stretches out, it looks like it is measuring something!

1. Where are the inchworm's legs?
2. Why do you think the middle of the inchworm's body goes up?
3. How long do you picture an inchworm being?
4. Why do you think an inchworm doesn't use its front and back legs at the same time?
5. How do you think the inchworm might have got its name?

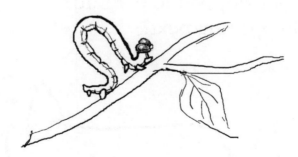

Level One

12.

Bud, the wiener dog, stood on his hind legs. He put his front paws up on the first step. Then he pulled his back legs up after him. He looked up at the stairs way above him and barked.

Bud put his paws on the second step. His back legs followed, and up and up and up he went. Finally, Bud was at the top. He was tired and panting.

Bud barked and wagged his tail when he saw Gran. Gran said, "Hello Bud," and walked right past him down the stairs. Bud looked sadly down the long flight of stairs and barked again.

1. What did you picture Bud doing when he got to the top?
2. Why do you think Bud might have wanted go up the stairs?
3. Why do you think Bud had a hard time getting up the stairs?
4. Why might Gran have not stopped to pet Bud?
5. What can you picture happening next?

Level Two

Level Two

1.

five sentences

Brad filled the bathtub with water very near the top. He put in all his toy boats, but there was not much room for him. He stepped into the bath and sat down. His biggest boat spilled over the side and onto the floor. Water splashed just as his mother opened the door to the bathroom.

1. What did you picture Brad putting in the bathtub?
2. Why do you think Brad filled the bathtub so full?
3. Why do you think he sat down carefully?
4. How do you think his mother will feel when she sees the bathroom?
5. What do you visualize happening next?

2.

five sentences

The Zuni Indians live in hot desert lands. They raise corn and sheep. There is little rain for the farms. The Zuni make strings of red, blue, black, and yellow beads. The Zuni love to wear their beads and dance to help make it rain.

1. What did you picture for where the Zuni Indians live?
2. Why do you think the Zuni may not be able to raise a lot of crops?
3. Why do you think they dance to make rain?
4. Do you think the beads are important to the Zuni? Why?
5. What is the main idea of all this imagery?

3.

Kim tiptoed to the pen where the little yellow ducks slept. She opened the white wooden gate. Then she clicked her tongue and threw the ducks some grain. The baby ducks woke up and shook their feathers. They raced over to peck at the grain, wiggling their little tails.

1. What did you picture sleeping in the pen?
2. Why did Kim tiptoe to the pen if she was just going to wake the baby ducks up?
3. Why do you think Kim clicked her tongue?
4. Why do you think the ducks shook their feathers?
5. What problem might Kim have had if the gate was left open?

4.

The walking stick is an insect. He has a long stick-like body with no wings. He also has stick arms and legs. He can grow to over a foot in length. The walking stick fools predators into thinking he is part of a tree.

1. What did you picture for the arms and legs of the walking stick.
2. Why can the walking stick make predators think he is part of a tree?
3. Do you think the walking stick makes a lot of movement when he sees a predator? Why or why not?
4. Do you think it is good or bad for a walking stick to grow over a foot long? Explain.
5. What would be a good title for all this imagery?

Level Two

5.

five sentences

Bumblebees are large yellow and black bees. They make their nests in the ground. They have big bodies and very small wings. Experts say bumblebees are so fat they should not be able to fly. They fly from flower to flower in beautiful gardens.

1. Where did you picture bumblebees making their nests?
2. Why might bumblebees make their nests in the ground?
3. Why do you think experts think that bumblebees shouldn't be able to fly?
4. What might happen to a bumblebee if it loses one wing?
5. What is the main idea of all these images?

6.

five sentences

Yucca plants live in deserts. They can store water in their thin pointed leaves that seem to come right out of the ground. In the center they have a big white or purple flower. The flower only opens at night. Moths come out at night and they love the yucca plant.

1. Where do yucca plants live?
2. Why is it important for a yucca plant to be able to store water?
3. Why do you think its flower may only come out at night?
4. Why might the Yucca plant only have one flower?
5. Why might moths love the yucca plant?
6. What is a good title for all this imagery?

7.

Many starfish are orange and have five arms. They are the shape of a star and they do not swim. The starfish holds on to rocks underwater. If it loses an arm, it quickly grows a new one.

1. What did you visualize for the color of most starfish?
2. Why do you think a starfish is called a starfish?
3. Why do you think a starfish can't swim?
4. How do you think a starfish might lose an arm?
5. Why might a starfish need to grow an arm back quickly?

8.

Dill stood at the edge of the lake trying to skip a rock over the top of the water. Each round rock he threw splashed once and sank. Then he heard his father calling for him. He had not been able to skip one rock, and now it was time to go home! Sad and mad, he kicked the ground and a small flat rock skipped over the top of the water.

1. What was the shape of the rocks Dill was trying to skip over the water?
2. Why do you think the rocks Dill threw would not skip?
3. Why do you think flat rocks might skip across the water better than round ones?
4. How do you think Dill felt after he kicked the rock and it skipped over the water?
5. What can you picture happening next?

Level Two

9.

five sentences

Short, heavy, brown aardvarks live in Africa. The aardvark uses long claws and feet with webs to dig in anthills. Its long nose and sticky tongue catch many ants and termites. The aardvark is slow and has large ears like a rabbit. It is also shy and only comes out at night.

1. What did you picture for the aardvark's nose and tongue?
2. Why do you think the aardvark's long claws might be a help to it?
3. Why might it be important for the aardvark to have a sticky tongue?
4. Why might an aardvark only come out at night?
5. Do you think the aardvark is a good fighter? Why or why not?

10.

five sentences

A hungry little gray squirrel looked for nuts under a tree. The grass was tall and green. The squirrel found only one nut. Just then, a big fat squirrel came up and grabbed the nut. The little squirrel chattered loudly at the thief, who dropped the nut and ran away.

1. Where was the little squirrel looking for nuts?
2. Why do think the little squirrel was looking for nuts in the grass and not in the tree?
3. How do you think the little squirrel felt when he finally found one nut?
4. Who was the thief and why do you think chattering might have made him drop the nut?
5. What could you picture happening next?

11.

The first handmade paper was called papyrus. This paper was made a long time ago from tall river reeds. First, men in a boat cut the reeds down. Ashore, the soft middle part was cut into thin strips and put in water.

The wet strips were placed criss-cross in layers. A big rock was laid on top until the layers dried. The dry sheets of paper were now ready to write on. Some papyrus sheets were very long. These were made into scrolls (sheets rolled into a tube).

1. What part of the papyrus did you picture being cut and soaked?
2. Why do you think they didn't use the outside of the reeds?
3. Why do you think the strips were crisscrossed?
4. Why do you think a weight was left on until the strips dried?
5. What problems do you picture happening if we still made paper like this?

Level Two

12.
two paragraphs

An old man held the string of a kite that was flying high up in the stormy sky. A lightning bolt flashed, followed by a mighty roar of thunder. The old man waited in the rain.

The old man moved his finger close to a large brass key tied to the kite string. Just as he was about to touch the key, a white spark jumped from the key to the old man's finger. Ben Franklin jerked his hand back in surprise and then he laughed. He had just proven that lightning is electricity.

1. What did you picture the night sky looking like?
2. Why do you think Ben Franklin was flying a kite in the rain?
3. Why do you think Franklin jerked his hand when he felt the spark?
4. Why do you think Franklin laughed when the sparks flew from the key to his finger?
5. Do you think that his flying the kite that night had an effect on you? Explain.

Some primal termite knocked on wood
And tasted it, and found it good!
And that is why your Cousin May
Fell through the parlor floor today.

—Ogden Nash

Level Three

Level Three

1. four sentences

Grandpa Joe was sitting on a red blanket under a tree at a picnic. He thought he saw a long brown stick in the green grass and he reached for it. Just then the stick slithered away from him. He thought to himself that it was very funny that a stick could move so fast.

    1. What color did you picture the blanket?
    2. Why do you think Grandpa Joe might have reached for a stick in the grass?
    3. What do you think the stick really was?
    4. Do you think Grandpa Joe knew the stick was a snake? Explain.
    5. What is a good title for all this imagery?

2. five sentences

The little goldfish swam slowly around in his bowl. Two huge blue eyes looked in. The goldfish calmly blew a bubble. Then a furry paw touched the surface of the water. The goldfish zipped into his castle and peeked out.

    1. What color did you picture the eyes that looked in the bowl?
    2. Who or what do you think was looking into the bowl?
    3. Why do you think the eyes looking in did not seem to bother the goldfish?
    4. Why do you think the paw touching the water did bother the goldfish?
    5. What problem might the goldfish have if his bowl of water had been shallow?

3. five sentences

There is a small bird that wags its tail like a puppy. The wagtail moves its long tail feathers almost all the time. The wagtail has a yellow belly and dark feathers. It continues to wag its tail while pecking the ground for insects and worms. When people see it, they just think it is a happy bird.

    1. What did you visualize for the wagtail's tail?
    2. How might its tail feathers call attention to the bird?
    3. Why do you think it might move its tail when it is pecking the ground?
    4. Why do you think people might think the wagtail is happy?
    5. What do you think it might mean if a wagtail stops wagging its tail?

4.

Ken wanted to be in the school band, but he had no instrument. His uncle gave him a tuba, but it had a ball stuck in it. His aunt found an old trombone, but it was bent almost in half. His dad brought home a piano, but it was missing half its keys. Ken thanked them all and finally joined the school choir.

1. What was stuck in the tuba?
2. Do you think Ken had a lot of money? Explain.
3. Why did Ken finally joined the choir?
4. What can you picture happening next?
5. What is a good title for all this imagery?

5.

The elephant uses its long muscular nose, called a trunk, to grab things. The trunk is strong enough to lift a man off the ground. It can also gently pick a dime up off the floor. An elephant has more muscles in its trunk than in all the rest of its body. Elephants use their trunks for many things, such as getting tree branches to eat and squirting water on themselves to stay cool.

1. What part of the elephant is its nose?
2. Why is it so surprising that the elephant's trunk has more muscles than the rest of his body?
3. Why do you think the elephant's trunk can lift something heavy and also pick up something small on the floor?
4. Why do you think the elephant has more muscles in its trunk than anywhere else?
5. Why might an elephant need to have a strong trunk to survive?

6.

People in the old days used to worry if the gold coins they used for money were real or fake. Then a miner found a special black stone, called a touchstone. Metals that were rubbed on the stone left different marks. Pure gold left a yellow mark like no other metal. Now people could test their gold coins.

1. What color did you picture the touchstone?
2. Why might different metals leave different marks on touchstone?
3. Why would people worry whether their gold was real or fake?
4. Where do you think touchstones were probably found? Why?
5. Why would people test their coins?

Level Three

7. six sentences

Kelly, an artist, sat in the park with a pad of white paper. Jack, a little boy with red hair, was playing on the grass. Kelly began to draw with short, quick strokes. After a few minutes, she called the little boy over. When she handed Jack the picture, he looked puzzled. Then he turned to the artist and giggled.

1. What color was little Jack's hair?
2. Why do you think the artist chose to draw Jack?
3. Do you think the boy knew he was being drawn?
4. Why do you think Jack giggled?
5. What is a good title for all this imagery?

8. five sentences

Ants live and work together in colonies. Each ant has its own special job to do. The huge queen ant lays eggs her entire life. Worker ants take care of the eggs, collect food, and feed the queen. Soldier ants have huge jaws and protect the colony from danger.

1. Where do you picture the ants living?
2. Why might ants live in colonies?
3. Why do you think the queen has to be fed?
4. Why might soldier ants have been given the name "soldier"?
5. Why are soldier ants perfect for protecting the colony?

9. four sentences

A comet is a ball of ice, dust, and gases orbiting the sun. As a comet nears the sun, the ice melts. The dust and gases stream out behind forming what looks like a long tail. Some comets come so close to Earth that people can see the tail of the comet.

1. What happens to a comet as it nears the sun?
2. Why do you think a comet's ice melts?
3. Why do you think the comet looks like it has a tail?
4. How do you think people a long time ago might have felt when they saw a comet? Why?
5. What is the main idea of all this imagery?

10.

The small brown head of an animal with bright eyes pops out of a hole in the hot red dirt of Africa. It is a meerkat, only one foot long, out to catch some warm sun. The cute meerkats lay on the sand to soak up the heat from the sun. They take turns hopping up to sniff the air for danger. It sleeps cuddled with its large family in a small safe burrow.

1. What do you picture for the size of the meerkat?
2. Why do you think the meerkats sleep in a burrow?
3. Why do you think meerkats take turns sniffing the air for danger?
4. What might happen to a meerkat if it gets too far away from its family?
5. What is the main idea of all this imagery?

11.

Jellyfish are a type of sea animal that floats in the water. Jellyfish can be as small as a pea. They can be as wide across as seven feet. Their whole body is made of a substance that looks like jelly. Jellyfish are colorful, like pink, orange, and blue.

Most jellyfish look like a bell or cup. Their dangling arms hang down from the body. The jellyfish pushes upward in water with its body. Then it floats back down to the floor of the sea.

On its way to the bottom, its arms catch little animals and fish. The jellyfish arms have tiny stinging spines. They can often hurt people if they are touched or stepped on. Some jellyfish, like the sea wasp, have a deadly sting and can kill you.

1. What did you picture for how the jellyfish swims in the ocean?
2. Why are the arms of the jellyfish important to it?
3. Why might people not be careful when they see a jellyfish?
4. Why might someone step on a jellyfish?
5. How do you think the sea wasp got its name?

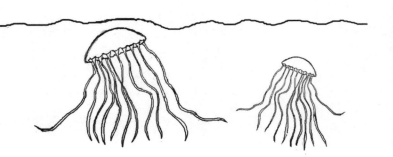

Level Three

12.

A volcano is a vent in the Earth. Deep inside our planet, it is very hot. The melted rock at the center is called magma. When a deep enough hole forms in the crust of the Earth, the magma and hot gas rush out as lava.

There are different types of lava. Some volcanoes pour out hot gas and ashes. Others pour out red-hot lava. Some even spit up big rocks and dirt.

When the volcano blows, it leaves a crater. Sometimes the inside of the crater is huge. After many years, the volcano becomes cold and plants might grow all over it. A crater might fill up with water and become a lake. But sometimes the volcano erupts again.

    1. What is the name of the melted rock in the center of our planet?
    2. Now that you've imaged this story, explain what is meant by "the volcano is a vent in the Earth."
    3. Why might a crater be formed?
    4. What might make a lake scary?
    5. What problems might there be if a volcano erupts after being dormant for hundreds of years?

There was an old man from Calcutta
Who coated his tonsils with butta
Thus converting his snore
From a thunderous roar
To a soft, oleaginous mutta.

-Ogden Nash

Level Four

Level Four

five sentences

1.

Quicksand is a mix of water and sand in big hole in the ground. The quicksand looks safe because you can't see the hole underneath it. But it is not safe, because it pulls animals or people down if they step on it. The best way to stop from being pulled down is to stay very still on the top. Walk carefully if you see sand on the ground, as it might not hold you up.

     1. What is quicksand a mixture of?
     2. Why would an animal or a person step in quicksand?
     3. What can you picture happening if someone struggles when they get stuck in quicksand?
     4. Do you think most animals or people stay still when they get stuck in quicksand? Why or why not?
     5. What is the main idea of all this imagery?

five sentences

2.

The three children ran down the long rows of apple trees in the orchard. They stopped in front of a towering Granny Smith apple tree. The huge green apples weighed heavily on the branches and bent them almost to the ground. The children filled their bags with the shiny green fruit. Then they headed for home with their mouths watering.

     1. How many children did you picture running?
     2. Why do you think the children ran through the orchard?
     3. If the apples were so heavy why didn't the branches break?
     4. Why do you think the children's mouths were watering?
     5. What is a good title for all this imagery?

five sentences

3.

Sara walked through the dirt streets of Babylon to the enormous temple. She looked up at the tall stone pillar in front of the temple. It was the pillar that had the Code of Hammurabi carved into it. The Code of Hammurabi was the first set of written laws. Sara had come to see what the law said about someone who steals a cow.

     1. What was the Code of Hammurabi carved into?
     2. Why do you think the Code was carved into the stone?
     3. Why do you think the laws were displayed in public for all to see?
     4. What do you think had happened to Sara that made her go to the temple?
     5. What can you picture happening next?

4.

Sharks are hunters that every fish fears. But they have travel buddies as they swim the seas in search of the next meal. Little brave fish called suckerfish swim right up to the deadly shark. They eat the fungus that can grow on a shark's sleek body. In return for cleaning service, the shark does not have the suckerfish for dinner.

1. What is the name of the shark's travel buddy?
2. Why do you think the story called suckerfish brave?
3. Why do you think it might be good for a shark not to have fungus on its body?
4. How do you think suckerfish got their name?
5. What might be a good title for all your images?

5.

Spanish moss grows in trees in the southern part of the United States. The moss wraps itself around the branches and hangs down like cobwebs. Warm breezes lift and twirl the mossy strands. On a stormy winter night when the moon is full, the moss looks like ghosts dancing in the trees. Graceful trees with Spanish moss are often seen on postcards showing off the beauty of the South.

1. What part of the United States has Spanish moss?
2. Why do you think Spanish moss might look like cobwebs?
3. Why do you think a stormy night and full moon might make the moss look like ghosts dancing?
4. Do you think Spanish moss is considered pretty? Why or why not?
5. What is the main idea?

Level Four

6.

Bones are an important part of every body. They form the basic shape of a human. More than 200 bones make up a single skeleton. Bones can grow, and they can break. Inside the body, bones are wrapped up in blue-red muscles and pink flesh. Outside of the body bones look white and feel brittle and dry. With no bones to hang the body on, a person would be just a lump.

1. How many bones are in a skeleton?
2. Why is it important that bones can grow?
3. Why might it help bones to be wrapped in muscles?
4. What might cause a bone to break?
5. Why would a person be just a lump with no bones? Would that be good or bad? Explain.

7.

Alaska is full of huge ice glaciers that reach so high they could be mountains of clouds. Great chunks of ice sit on the water like pieces of a broken mirror. The bright yellow sun flares over the ice and turns it into a field of sparkling diamonds. Often white seals sleep and play on the ice with their babies. However, sometimes a close big pile of snow is really a hunting polar bear. Then the seals have to scatter for safety.

1. What did you picture for the glaciers?
2. Why do you think the polar bear might be able to get close to the seals?
3. What makes it so hard to see the bear?
4. Why might glaciers look like "a field of sparkling diamonds"?
5. What can you predict happening next to the seals and the polar bear?

8.

The mockingbird is a very clever bird. She got her name by being able to copy any birdcall she hears. She also lays her eggs in other birds' nests rather than build her own. Her chicks might then be raised with other birds. These foster parent birds cannot really tell that the little brown bird chick looks different than their own chicks. The mockingbird is so clever that she can even fool other birds into raising her babies!

    1. What kind of bird is this story about?
    2. Why might it benefit the mockingbird to copy other birdcalls?
    3. Why might a mockingbird want to have other birds raise its babies?
    4. Why do you think mockingbird is a good name for this bird?

9.

Some redwood forests have stood for hundreds of years. The trees grow very tall and block out most of the sun. The tree trunks can grow wider than a bus. Under the umbrella of each tree's wide branches grow lush green ferns and mosses. The cool damp air is perfect for the delicate unrolled arms of the ferns that root at the redwood's base.

    1. How long do some redwood trees live?
    2. What problems could be caused by no sunlight coming in a forest?
    3. What could be some benefits to no sunlight coming in?
    4. What might happen if a tree wider than a bus fell down?
    5. What might happen to the forest if all the redwood trees were cut or had fallen down?

Level Four

10.

five sentences

It was late in the evening. Hot air had settled over the swamp like a thick blanket. An alligator slipped under the flat surface of the water with a silent splash. He likes to hunt at night. It was a good night for the alligator because the cool swamp was full of a type of fish called the pink-bellied bass.

1. What sound did you hear when the alligator went into the water?
2. Why do you think an alligator hunts at night?
3. Why do you think the alligator slipped into the water silently rather than with a loud splash?
4. What do you think the alligator was going after?
5. Why do you think it was a good night for the alligator?

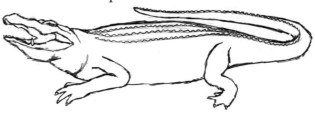

11.

two paragraphs

In 1903, on a cold and icy winter morning, Wilbur and Orville Wright tested their flying project. Their experimental biplane was made of wood and canvas. It had two flimsy sets of wings. Orville was strapped to the frame.

The engine roared and the plane moved along a wooden track. When it reached the end of the track, it rose slowly into the air and flew. The Wright brothers were the first in history to make a motorized flight—which lasted only 12 seconds!

1. What was the biplane made of?
2. Why do you think the plane was made of wood and not metal?
3. Why was Orville strapped to the plane?
4. Why do you think the plane ran along a wooden track instead of on the ground?
5. Even though it was very short, was the Wright brothers' first flight important?

12.

When gold was discovered in California in 1849, thousands raced west to strike it rich. They used pans and sieves to look for gold in the rivers. They swung picks and dug with shovels to search for gold in the hills.

Only a few of the people looking for gold got rich. Some of the people who got the richest weren't looking for gold at all. They made huge fortunes selling supplies to the gold miners. The miners who did not find gold either found other work or returned home.

    1. What numbers did you picture for the year gold was discovered in California?
    2. Why did so many people rush to California?
    3. Why do you think people rushed to get gold?
    4. Why could people make huge fortunes selling supplies?
    5. What do you think happened to the miners who returned home without gold?

Level Five

Level Five

1. five sentences

For weeks, Gina got messy painting the set while the actors practiced their lines for the school play. On the night of the play, one of the stars came down with a bad cold and couldn't perform. Gina suddenly realized that from being at every rehearsal she knew all the lines—and volunteered to fill in. After the play, Gina was told she would not be allowed to paint sets next year. When she asked why, she was told she would be too busy starring in the play.

1. What did you visualize Gina doing while the actors practiced?
2. Why might a cold keep someone out of a play?
3. Why might Gina know all the lines?
4. Why was she going to star in the play?
5. What is a good title for all this imagery?

2. five sentences

Despite living on remote islands, the dodo bird is now extinct. This squat fowl could grow to weigh 50 pounds. The dodo was fat like a turkey, but with such tiny wings that it could not fly. With no natural enemies, the dodo had no instinctive fear. Sailors who stopped at the remote islands simply walked up and caught the trusting birds where they stood—and the dodo soon disappeared.

1. How much could a dodo bird weigh?
2. How might living on a remote island help an animal not become extinct?
3. What about the dodo bird made it vulnerable on remote islands?
4. Why was it easy for a human to catch a dodo bird?
5. Who was the enemy of the dodo bird? Explain.

3.

The lights dimmed in the theater, hidden drums began to pound, and the masked dancers snaked through the audience. Suddenly, a man in a lion mask leaped, crouching, onto the stage. The long yellow hair around his mask swayed gently as the lion dancer looked back and forth. In a moment, the other dancers in their colorful animal masks began to circle around him. The audience was enthralled with the beauty of each movement. No one moved or even dared to breathe until the performance was over.

    1. What color did you picture for the hair around the lion mask?
    2. Why do you think the dancers moved through the audience?
    3. Why do you think the man with the lion mask looked back and forth?
    4. Why do you think the other dancers circled the man with the lion mask?
    5. What would be a good title for the imagery in this story?

4.

Dr. Livingstone stumbled into an African village, weak and sick. He had been searching for the source of the Nile River. The kind people of the village took him in and cared for him. One day, a few years later, a man strode calmly out of the thick jungle into the village and asked, "Dr. Livingstone, I presume?" The man was a newspaper reporter sent to find Dr. Livingstone. No one had really expected him to find Dr. Livingstone deep in the jungle.

    1. What river was Dr. Livingstone trying to find the source of?
    2. Why might Dr. Livingstone have stayed in the village so long?
    3. Why might it be hard to find someone deep in a jungle?
    4. Why do you think the reporter was sent to find Dr. Livingstone if no one really thought he would succeed?
    5. What might you picture happening next?

Level Five

5.

One day after school, Carl was starting for home when his bike chain broke. It lay on the ground like a dead metal snake. Carl looked up at the steep hill, and picked a new way home. On this new route, Carl discovered a store that sold old comic books, a movie theater that only showed old science fiction movies, and a magic shop. Carl thought he just might have to break his chain again sometime.

1. What happened to Carl's bicycle?
2. Why do you think Carl took a new way home?
3. Why do you think Carl didn't know about the shops and the theater already?
4. Do you think Carl might be happy that his chain broke? Why?
5. Why did Carl think he might break his bike chain again?

6.

Jill was eating in a very fancy restaurant with her parents for the first time. She carefully laid the stiff starched cloth napkin across her lap. When the waiter slid a salad in front of her, she picked up the correct fork; the smaller, wider one. She watched as the waiter cranked black pepper out of a giant pepper grinder. Then she watched as the waiter started to pour more ice water into the elegant glasses. Suddenly, Jill's napkin slid off her lap and she bent down to get it just as the waiter leaned forward—bump!

1. What did you picture Jill dropping?
2. Why do you think Jill watched the waiter so closely?
3. What did you picture Jill bumping?
4. What did you picture happening after the bump?
5. What is a good title for all this imagery?

7.

When Sarah woke up, her room was much brighter with sunshine than usual. She yawned and rubbed her eyes, and then saw that her clock had stopped. Afraid she was in trouble again, Sarah jumped out of bed and ran to look at her wristwatch that was sitting on the dresser. She couldn't believe her eyes; it was after nine o'clock! Sarah quickly slid out of her pink striped pajamas, pulled on a blue dress, grabbed her schoolbooks, and rushed out of the house.

1. What did Sarah see when she woke up?
2. What do you think happened that made Sarah's clock stop?
3. Why do you think the wristwatch was working right?
4. Do you think this had happened to Sarah before? Explain.
5. Where do you think Sarah went in such a hurry?

8.

When pioneers reached the Great Plains in their covered wagons, they discovered there were very few trees to cut for houses. The clever pioneers learned to cut blocks of sod, a layer of ground with grass on it, out of the earth for building. The blocks were stacked to make walls. Boards from a wagon were used for roof rafters, and blocks of sod were placed on top to give the house a green grass roof. Rain rolled right off the grass roof, and the pioneer family was safe and snug in their sod house.

1. Where did you picture the pioneers in this story?
2. Why do you think they used sod to build their homes?
3. What problems do you think there might be with a house made of sod?
4. What do you think might have happened if the pioneers put the blocks on the roof dirt side up?
5. Why might rain "roll off" a grass roof?

Level Five

9.

two paragraphs

Snowboarding is one of the newest Olympic sports, and also one of the craziest. The snowboarders wear baggy oversized winter clothes. They ride with both feet locked into place on a snowboard that looks like a miniature surfboard. One by one, they fly down a hill and swoop into a giant snow-walled ditch called a half-pipe.

A half-pipe looks like a giant length of pipe with the top half sliced right off. As the riders shoot up the side of the half-pipe, they seem to pause in mid air. They do complicated twists and somersaults in the air before they hurtle back down. If all goes well, the rider slides back down the side of the half pipe, right up the other side, and into the air again.

1. What does a snowboard look like?
2. Why might the rider's feet be locked onto the board?
3. Why do you think they snowboard one by one and not all at once?
4. Why would a half-pipe shape be a good way to get the rider airborne?
5. What is a good title for all the imagery in this story?

10.

three paragraphs

Julie was making a big spaghetti dinner for her family. She seasoned and stirred the spicy red tomato sauce just like she had learned in school. Then she boiled some water in a big steel pot, and put the long thin noodles in. When the noodles were soft and white, Julie picked up the heavy pot with two hot pads and carried it to the sink.

She held the lid almost closed as she slowly poured the water into the sink. Hot steam rose from the pot, and Julie was very careful. But steam fogged her glasses, and somehow the lid slipped. The noodles went sliding out into the soapy dishwater.

Julie let out a terrible wail, and her parents came running into the kitchen. When they saw what had happened, they began to laugh. They put the sauce in the refrigerator for another day. Then Julie and her parents went out to eat at a restaurant.

1. What kind of sauce did Julie make for the spaghetti?
2. Why would having your glasses get fogged make doing a job harder?
3. Why do you think Julie's parents ran into the room?
4. Why do you think Julie and her parents went out to eat instead of boiling more noodles?
5. What do you think they ordered at the restaurant? Why?

11.

High on a sturdy branch hidden away behind a mass of green leaves, Andy watched everyone scurrying around the back yard. He laughed quietly to himself. No one knew he was hidden in the tree.

Andy watched Uncle Bob flipping hamburgers on the grill. He saw Aunt Becky spread the red and white-checked tablecloth on the picnic table and then set out bowls of potato salad and baked beans. Dad set up the kids' card table and put paper plates, cups, napkins, and forks out all around. Andy saw everything.

Finally, Mom came out of the house carrying two big pitchers of iced tea and soda. She placed them on the table with the food. Then she looked up into the branches of the tree and said, "Andy, come down and wash your hands before you eat."

1. Where did you visualize Andy hiding?
2. Why do you think Andy was hiding?
3. Why did Andy think that no one knew he was in the tree?
4. Do you think Andy's mother knew where he was? Explain.
5. What might you visualize happening next?

12.

Sharp black outlines stand against the bright colors of the sunset. The breeze rolls a tumbleweed down the deserted main street. Wooden shutters flap against broken windows. The front door of an empty hotel is slowly falling off its hinges. Here and there in the jumble of the "ghost town" lean old wagon wheels.

Ruins of ghost towns dot the American West. This is all that remains of the gold and silver booms of the 1800's. During their heyday, towns with names like Calico and Bodie housed up to 10,000 hopeful miners. When the mines ceased to produce, people simply packed up and headed for the next boomtown. The buildings and equipment left behind are well preserved by the dry desert climate of the West.

1. Where did you picture ghost towns?
2. What do you think made the sharp black outlines in the first sentence?
3. Why do you think miners would leave equipment behind?
4. Why do you think the towns are called ghost towns?
5. Why it is so amazing that some ghost towns once had 10,000 people in them?

Tell me, O Octopus, I begs,

    Is those things arms or is they legs?

I marvel at thee, Octopus;

If I were thou, I'd call me Us.

-Ogden Nash

Level Six

Level Six

1. five sentences

It is just a simple gold locket, but it is priceless to Beth. It was a birthday gift from her grandmother nearly two years ago. Inside the locket, her grandmother placed two small photos—one of Beth and one of herself when she was a young girl. Beth always wears the locket next to her heart and never takes it off, not even to take a bath. When people see the photos, they ask her what it is like to be a twin.

    1. What color did you visualize the locket?
    2. Why do you think Beth's grandmother put the two pictures inside?
    3. Why didn't Beth's grandmother put in a recent picture of herself?
    4. Why do you think Beth wears the locket next to her heart?
    5. Why would people think Beth was a twin?

2. six sentences

Jackrabbits live in wild dry country and are brownish-gray like the brush where they make their homes. Their fur is rougher than the fur of the cute little bunnies people often get for pets. Jackrabbits' ears are extra-long and they hear extremely well. Their hind legs are also extra-long, making them very fast runners and high jumpers. Jackrabbits slip out of the thickest, most tangled part of the brush at dusk and dawn to search for food. They zigzag when they run, and even the wily coyote, the quickest and cleverest of hunters, needs the element of surprise to catch a jackrabbit.

    1. Where do you picture jackrabbits living?
    2. Why do you think jackrabbits are the same color as the brush?
    3. Why do you think they live in the thickest, most tangled part of the brush?
    4. Why do you think they only eat at dusk and dawn?
    5. What about the jackrabbit would make getting the element of surprise especially hard?

3.

At the ripe old age of 90, Ramses the Great, pharaoh of Egypt, died. A series of handmade wooden coffins, each one fitting inside the next, housed his mummified body. These were placed into a huge sarcophagus of stone inlaid with gold and precious jewels. A tomb was carved into a wall of rock in the desert Valley of Kings. Buried with Ramses were treasures and household items he might need in the afterlife.

1. What number did you picture for how old Ramses the Great was when he died?
2. Why might there be so many coffins for one mummified body?
3. Why do you think Ramses was not buried in a plain sarcophagus?
4. What do you think was in the Valley of the Kings?
5. Why do you think the Egyptians believed Ramses the Great might need treasures in the afterlife?

4.

Honeybees fly up to a mile from their hive to collect nectar from flowers. They carry the nectar back to the hive in a special "honey stomach." Inside the hive, they empty the nectar into six-sided wax honeycomb cells. The water in the nectar evaporates, leaving behind thick sweet honey. The cell is then capped off with more wax, and the honey is preserved in the cell as food for all the bees.

1. How far do you picture the honeybees flying for nectar?
2. Why would the bee have a special stomach?
3. How do you think honeybees empty their special stomachs?
4. Why wouldn't the honeybees just use one stomach for everything?
5. What is a good title for all these pictures?

Level Six

5. five sentences

Archaeologists digging near the Nile River in Africa have found riches from the once-mighty kingdom of Kush. Though the people left long ago, huge statues and immense temples remain. In graves, the diggers have found gold, ivory, and jewels. The people of Kush also built pyramids like those in Egypt. Inside the pyramids is Egyptian picture writing.

1. What was the name of the long-ago kingdom near the Nile River in Africa?
2. Why do you think archaeologists dig up old cities like this?
3. Why might the statues and temples still be there?
4. Why do you think the people of Kush buried gold and jewels in their graves?
5. Why do you think the people of Kush might have left?

6. six sentences

Tom and Bob spent the summer working on their uncle's farm. They were worried that it would be boring, but from morning until night there always seemed to be something to do on the farm. When they weren't feeding the cows, they were running the milking machines. When they weren't picking vegetables, they were hoeing weeds. By the end of the summer, Tom and Bob had learned a lot about animals, nutrition, and nature. From all the work out in the sun, they were tan and strong, and had a new respect for farmers.

1. What kind of machines did the boys learn to run?
2. Where do you think Tom and Bob lived? In the city or on a farm? Explain.
3. Why do you think they were worried about being bored?
4. Do you think the boys learned something different than they would have at home? Explain.
5. How do you think the boys thought about farmers before they went and why did it change?

7.

The earliest known mummies from Egypt were not placed in pyramids. Each was buried in a shallow grave in the sand of the desert. They date back to over 5,000 years ago, before writing was invented, so there are no records of who the mummies were when they were living people. The graves also contained things like necklaces and pots. The graves were unmarked in the shifting sands. The most famous sand mummy is nicknamed Ginger for his red hair.

1. What kind of things did you visualize placed in the graves?
2. Why do you think the graves were shallow?
3. What do you think might be difficult about burying a mummy in the desert sand?
4. How might people have discovered the graves if they were unmarked?
5. Why do you think there were things like necklaces in the graves?

8.

The first parachutes were made out of silk, but now they are constructed from nylon or from Kevlar, the same material as a bulletproof vest. The model for the parachute is the umbrella, and cords hang down from the edges of the umbrella to a harness strapped on a person. The cords are pulled to let air out one side of the canopy or the other to control the parachute. Parachutes can be round, but most now are wing shaped.

1. What were the first parachutes made out of?
2. Why do you think parachutes needed to be made of a very strong material like Kevlar?
3. Why do you think the early parachutes were round?
4. Why might a person using a parachute need to wear a harness?
5. Why might it be important to be able to control a parachute?

Level Six

9.

Leonardo da Vinci lived in 15th century Italy and built his life around art and learning. He was a very successful painter and sculptor. Many of his works of art, like the Mona Lisa, can still be seen in museums around the world. However, many of his works were never completed. He tried to make a huge bronze horse for the Duke of Milan. The horse was designed to be 20 feet high and would have weighed over 200,000 pounds. Unfortunately, this was too much for Leonardo. He only was able to make several models, which were later destroyed by war.

Leonardo da Vinci was also a scientist, engineer, and inventor. The left-handed artist filled hundreds of notebooks with his observations and designs. Interestingly, many of his notes can only be read with a mirror. He wrote his notes backwards and from right to left! He also left behind designs for submarines and flying machines hundreds of years before they would be built. It is no wonder he was called the most creative mind of his time.

    1. When and where did Leonardo da Vinci live?
    2. Why do you think he was unable to finish his sculpture of a bronze horse?
    3. Do you think studying science and architecture helped him become a better artist?
    4. Why do you think he wrote his notes in such an unusual manner?
    5. What is the main idea of this story?

10.

Nelson Mandela, a black man, grew up in South Africa. At that time, the people there were treated differently according to their skin color. The government made each racial group use separate schools, hospitals, and housing. Mandela became a lawyer and fought for equal rights for all people. In 1962, Mandela went to prison for 27 years for his protests against the government.

While he was in prison, people continued to protest and work for change. Mandela became a symbol of their cause. In 1990, the government finally released Mandela. He resumed his work for equality until the laws were eventually changed. At last, everyone had the same rights. One of these was the right to vote. In the first national election that was open to all people, Mandela was elected to be the first black president of South Africa.

    1. How long was Mandela imprisoned?
    2. Why do you think Mandela was kept in prison for so long?
    3. Do you think being in prison changed Mandela in any way?
    4. Why did Mandela go right back to his cause if it had gotten him jailed?
    5. Why is it an important event in history that Mandela became president of South Africa?

11.

The Mardi Gras celebration in New Orleans happens once a year in March. It is a nonstop street party. For several days, people in colorful costumes dance and parade through the city. They come from all over the world to join in. The event started long ago as competition between two groups of French settlers trying to make the most outlandish costumes.

Today at Mardi Gras, you will see many costumes covered in feathers, sequins, and beads. Other people caper about dressed as jesters or clowns. Some people dress normally and paint just their faces with wild colorful designs. The costumed people who ride the parade floats throw strings of bright beads to begging crowds.

    1. Who started the Mardi Gras?
    2. What kind of music did you picture accompanying the dancing and parading? Why?
    3. Why would people use feathers and beads on their costumes?
    4. How might some people paint their faces? Why?
    5. Why do you think the people on floats throw beads to the crowd?

12.

Jane was at the circus with her parents where they sat in the very front row, munching popcorn. There were sawdust and peanut shells under their feet. Jane stared up at the tall red circus tent towering over her. She saw the thin wire where the tightrope walker would later perform, and the tiny platforms the trapeze artists would leap from to fly through the air.

Then it was time for the opening parade. Trumpets blared and all the animals in the circus began to march right past her. She could smell and nearly touch the elephants, horses, and camels as they paraded by. Tigers and lions in red cages on wheels snarled and growled at the audience. It was amazing and even a little scary to see the wild animals so close up.

Suddenly, a small monkey in a red suit ran over to Jane. She was afraid but she found herself laughing. The little monkey ran up her legs and sat in her lap. He pointed to Jane's popcorn and chittered. Then he grabbed the bag and ran back to the parade!

    1. What row did Jane and her parents sit in?
    2. Why do you think there was sawdust under their feet?
    3. Why do you think Jane was scared?
    4. Why do you think Jane laughed?
    5. What is a good title for all this imagery?

Hark to the whimper of the sea-gull;

He weeps because he's not an ea-gull.

Suppose you were, you silly sea-gull.

Could you explain it to your she-gull?

—Ogden Nash

Level Seven

Level Seven

1.

A steady hum filled the air as the Hindenburg, a giant blimp, floated into view from behind the clouds. This monstrous dirigible was the pride of Germany. It had just carried 97 passengers across the Atlantic Ocean. As it prepared to land, the explosive hydrogen gas that kept it aloft somehow ignited. The Hindenburg burst into a mighty ball of smoke and flames and slowly fell to earth. Surprisingly, most of the passengers survived the crash. But no longer would the giant airships be used for transportation.

    1. What country was the Hindenburg from?
    2. What do you think it means that the Hindenburg was "the pride of Germany"? Explain.
    3. What do you think could have caused the Hindenburg to catch fire?
    4. How do you think so many people could have survived the flaming crash?
    5. Until the Hindenburg, people had to take ocean liners across the Atlantic Ocean. Name two things that would make people happier to take a dirigible.

2.

In late August, large groups of monarch butterflies begin to migrate south to Mexico or west to California. These huge groups often cluster together at night for protection from the cool fall temperatures. After traveling as much as 2000 miles, they reach the same trees their parents left the year before. There they stay until spring comes and they begin their long journey back. Next fall, it will be their children's turn because each butterfly can only make the round trip flight once.

    1. What kind of butterfly is the story about and how many miles do they travel?
    2. Why do you think they begin to migrate in late August?
    3. Why would clustering together at night protect them from the cool temperatures?
    4. How do you think they are able to find the same trees their parents stayed at the year before?
    5. What might be the reason they only make this trip once?

3.

In 17th century Britain, people sneezed to show boredom or disapproval. Since it is difficult to force a sneeze, wealthy people sniffed finely ground tobacco, called snuff. With snuff, a person could express disdain at any time. Just a tiny pinch was enough to cause an enormous sneeze. For many people, having a little tin of snuff with them was as necessary as having money or an umbrella. Snuff is no longer fashionable, but we still use the phrase "nothing to sneeze at" to mean something that is well done.

1. In 17th century Britain, what did you picture people doing to show they were bored or displeased?
2. Do you think snuff was cheap or expensive? Why?
3. Why might they carry snuff in a tin?
4. Why do you think it is that snuff is no longer fashionable?
5. What is the main idea of all these images?

4.

One of the myths of ancient Greece is the tragic story of a beautiful blonde boy named Narcissus. Narcissus was very conceited and wanted only to be with himself. One day the boy spotted his own reflection in a pool of water and fell so deeply in love with it that he refused to leave. He lay at the edge of the pond until he died, heartbroken that he could not get to the one he loved. To this day, we use the word "narcissistic" to describe people who are too pleased with their own appearance.

1. Where did you visualize Narcissus seeing his own reflection?
2. Narcissus loved his reflection in the pool, but wouldn't he have already seen himself in a mirror hundreds of times? Explain.
3. Narcissus loved staring at his reflection in the pool—what would happen if he put his hands in the water to hold or kiss it?
4. Do you think Narcissus had friends? Explain.
5. What might have happened if Narcissus fell in the water?

Level Seven

5.   five sentences

Sitting at the edge of a clearing in the African jungle, Jane Goodall watched a mother chimpanzee and her baby. With a notebook and pencil in her hand, Jane looked on silently as the baby grabbed fistfuls of his mother's fur. The mother never complained, and continued to cradle and sometimes tickle her infant. Jane smiled as she wrote down every action the family made, and then paused before adding one more line. "So like us," she wrote.

    1. Where did you visualize Jane Goodall as she watched the chimpanzees?
    2. Why do you think Jane Goodall was watching the chimpanzees?
    3. Why do you think Jane Goodall had a notebook and pencil?
    4. What do you think Jane Goodall meant by the words "so like us"?
    5. What is the main idea of this story?

6.   five sentences

The Parthenon was built 2,500 years ago on a tall rocky hill in Greece. During construction the area was a beehive of artisans, artists, and laborers. It took 15 years to build the great temple. To this day, tall white marble columns surround a plaza of statues and murals. The Parthenon was built to honor the goddess of wisdom, Athena.

    1. What was Athena the goddess of?
    2. What do you think it means that the site was a beehive of activity?
    3. Why do you think it took so many people so long to build the Parthenon?
    4. How might it be different if the temple was built today?
    5. Does the temple still exist? Explain how you can know.

7.

Elizabeth Blackwell became the first woman doctor in the United States fighting the odds all the way. Twenty-nine schools refused her before she landed at Geneva College. There she faced prejudice. She became a doctor, but she was barred from most hospitals and had few patients. In 1857, she and her younger sister, Emily, a surgeon, opened their own hospital, staffed with women. She spent her life mostly treating the poor of New York.

1. How many schools refused to admit Elizabeth Blackwell before she was accepted to Geneva College?
2. Why do you think Blackwell kept applying to schools after so many rejected her?
3. Why do you think she was barred from most hospitals?
4. Why do you think Blackwell and her sister opened their own hospital?
5. Why do you think Blackwell staffed her hospital with women?

8.

Sea otters have adapted to spending most of their lives on or below the surface of the northern Pacific Ocean. They rarely go on land except to give birth. An otter is well prepared for life in the sea with long thick outer fur, and an undercoating of shorter fur that traps air. Air trapped in this undercoating is warmed by body heat, and forms an insulated layer to keep the otter warm and dry in the cold water. An otter may look wet, but its skin is really as dry as that of any land animal.

A sea otter can hold its breath for as long as four minutes and dive to a depth of nearly 200 feet. Under the surface, it searches the ocean floor, turning over rocks with its sharp claws. When the otter finds a tasty clam to eat, it carries the clam and a rock to the surface. Floating on its back, the sea otter balances the rock on its belly and holds the clam in its grasping paws. Then it smashes the clam against the rock until the shell breaks and the otter can pick out the meat inside. When it is time to sleep, which an otter also does on its back, it will wrap itself in the long, strong strands of a floating kelp bed to keep from drifting.

1. What ocean did you visualize otters living in?
2. Why do you think an otter goes on land to give birth?
3. Why is it important that a sea otter can hold its breath a long time? Explain.
4. How big do you think a rock would have to be for an otter to crack a clamshell on it?
5. What would make a sleeping otter drift if it did not wrap up in kelp?

Level Seven

9.   two paragraphs

Babe Didrikson sat alone on the grass as she began to stretch and prepare for the day's track and field events. All around her were large teams of women athletes competing at the National AAU track and field championships. But Babe was the only person on her team and she was about to compete in eight different events in one afternoon.

Babe ran from event to event, stopping only to get her equipment or wait for her next turn. As the afternoon raced by, Babe collected medal after medal. By the end of the day, Babe had won six events. She had also won the team championship single-handed, beating the other team, which had twenty members, by eight points. Soon her name would be known worldwide.

1. How many members were on Babe's team?
2. Why do you think Babe was going to compete in eight different events?
3. What might be a reason that Babe didn't win all eight of her events?
4. Do you think Babe needed more people on her team? Explain.
5. Why do you think Babe would become famous worldwide?

10.   two paragraphs

Through the dark moonless night, a group of frightened people moved through the heavy forest careful not to make a sound. They were escaped slaves and the Underground Railroad, a network of safe houses and guides, was taking them to freedom. Each step was dangerous as slave hunters searched the entire area with bloodhounds. If the escaped slaves were found, they would be taken back to their owners in chains. With only the North Star to guide them, the group continued to quickly move.

After going about 15 miles, their guide, or conductor as she was called, motioned for the group to follow her to a small white house at the edge of the forest. While they waited hidden among the scratchy bushes, the conductor went to the back door and quietly knocked. No one dared to move or breathe until they saw the signal that all was clear and they could enter the house. The family inside welcomed everyone and gave each person hot food and dry clothes. Then the exhausted group was taken to a secret room hidden in the back of the house. There they could rest until the night came and it was safe to move to the next home and eventually to freedom.

1. Who were the people in the group and where were they going?
2. Was the Underground Railroad really a train? Explain.
3. Why was it called the Underground Railroad?
4. Why was the guide called a conductor?
5. What were the "stops" on the Underground Railroad?

11.

Simon Bolivar, inspired by the American Revolution, led South America to freedom from Spain. Spain taxed the people in its colonies heavily, which kept most of them very poor. The people became more and more angry and began to organize violent uprisings. Spain, not wanting to give up its colonies, sent large armies to South America.

Simon Bolivar was not a soldier, but he took command of a patriot army in 1810, and proved to be natural leader. At first, the Spanish armies beat his army, but Bolivar learned from his losses. He began to win battles and was able to free six colonies from Spanish rule. Colonies formed new countries that chose Simon Bolivar as their president. One colony that became a country was named Bolivia in his honor. Simon Bolivar, the hero who freed thousands of people, is often called the George Washington of South America.

1. What inspired Bolivar to want to free South America from Spain?
2. Why do you think the American Revolution was inspiring?
3. Why do you think Spain did not want to lose its colonies?
4. Why do you think Bolivar took command if he was not a soldier?
5. What might have happened if Simon Bolivar hadn't come along or been born?

Level Seven

12.

Jackie wanted to play basketball, but her brother and sister said she was too small to play with them. One day, Jackie's mother saw her sitting on the gray concrete steps watching as the others played. Her mother leaned down and quietly whispered in Jackie's ear, "Why don't you practice when they aren't at home? Then you can get really good and show them that you are good enough to play."

After that, every afternoon Jackie would pick up the basketball and practice. She practiced dribbling with her left hand and with her right. She practiced lay-ups and free-throws. She practiced until she could make a basket from anywhere on the driveway.

The next time her brother and sister played basketball, Jackie asked them to let her play, too. Her brother took the ball to a spot at the far edge of the driveway and said, "If you can make a basket from here, then you can play." Jackie bounced the orange and black ball two times, lined up her shot, and let it sail towards the basket. Swwiiiisssh was the sound the ball made as it fell through the hoop, touching nothing but the net.

1. Why wouldn't Jackie's brother and sister let her play basketball?
2. Why do you think she practiced dribbling with both her left and right hands?
3. Why do you think Jackie's brother and sister told her to shoot from the far edge of the driveway?
4. What might you visualize happening next?

Behold the hippopotamus!

We laugh at how he looks to us,

And yet in moments dark and grim,

I wonder how we look to him.

Peace, peace, thou hippopotamus!

We really look all right to us,

As you no doubt delight the eye

Of other hippopotami.

—Ogden Nash

Level Eight

Level Eight

six sentences

1.

Women made many contributions to the American Revolutionary War effort. Some became nurses for the army and helped tend wounded soldiers. Other women went with their husbands to the battlefields to cook meals and sew for the men. Others, who stayed home, took over the jobs that men had normally done. A few women disguised themselves as men and actually fought in the army. Because they could travel freely, a few women became highly skilled spies who gathered information about the British.

    1. What war effort was named in the story?
    2. Do you think the women who became nurses had to go to nurse school first? Explain.
    3. Why do you think women had to disguise themselves in order to fight?
    4. Why do you think women were allowed to travel freely?
    5. Why do you think women in those days might never have been suspected of spying?

four sentences

2.

The mythical basilisk was said to be a giant scaly lizard with the head and wings of a rooster. The fearsome creature existed only to kill, which it could do with its piercing and fatal gaze, or its lethal breath. If a brave warrior managed to somehow spear a basilisk, its poisonous blood would travel up the spear and kill the attacker. According to legend, the only way a basilisk could die was if it gazed upon its own hideous image in a mirror.

    1. What did a basilisk have the head and wings of?
    2. What might it be about a basilisk looking at someone that would kill them?
    3. Why might its breath be able to kill?
    4. Why might a spear do better than a sword to kill a basilisk?
    5. Why do you think a basilisk would die if it looked in a mirror?

3.

Binti Jua is a lowland gorilla and a very special hero. One day a three-year-old boy fell 18 feet into the gorilla enclosure at the Brookfield Zoo near Chicago. Nervous spectators rushed around to see what would happen. The zoo staff quickly ran to the enclosure, but Binti was the first to reach the boy. With her own baby on her back, Binti cradled the unconscious boy and gently carried him to the door where the zoo staff was waiting. The little boy was taken to the hospital where he recovered from his fall.

1. Who is Binti Jua?
2. Why do you think Binti is called a hero?
3. Why might the spectators have been nervous?
4. Why do you think Binti carried the little boy to the door?
5. Why do you think Binti didn't hurt the boy?

4.

The submarine is a marvel of modern science, but it wasn't always safe or practical. The first time someone tried to build one, they used two wooden boats, one on top of the other, wrapped in leather. It wasn't watertight, and there was no air to breathe. The Turtle, the first combat sub, used in the Revolutionary War, was egg-shaped, made of wood, and had a hand-cranked propeller. It could only go underwater for a short time. When inventors solved the problems of power and air by using electricity and built a submarine out of metal, it finally became possible to travel underwater for long distances. Since then, subs, able to sneak around and under warships, have played an important role in every major war.

1. What was the name of the sub used in the Revolutionary War?
2. What do you think happened to the person who tested the first sub?
3. Why does a sub require an air source?
4. Do you think the propeller on the Turtle was very effective? Explain.
5. How would submarines be helpful in wartime?

Level Eight

5.

six sentences

The Mahikans were one of many American Indian tribes in Northeast America long ago. Their home was woodlands where black bear, deer, moose, beaver, otter, and bobcats roamed the forest. Mahikan men fished the rivers in hand-carved canoes with spears and nets. Children helped their mothers in gardens, where they grew vegetables like squash. They stored dried food in deep pits dug into the ground. Their wigwams were made of curved and tied saplings and hung with dried animal hides, or longhouses made of stacked logs that held whole clans.

1. What part of America did the Mahikans live in?
2. Why might it be important that so many animals were in the forest?
3. Why do you think the Mahikans dug deep pits in the ground?
4. Why might dried food last better in a pit than out in the open?
5. What is a good title for all this imagery?

6.

five sentences

Gum was an important part of every kid's life even in colonial times. Early settlers learned to chew a gum made from spruce trees from American Indians. Later settlers made gum from spruce wax mixed with beeswax. Candymakers added things like mint leaves or licorice to spice up the gum. It wasn't until 1906 that Frank Fleer invented a chewing gum that also blew bubbles, which he called Blibber-Blubber gum.

1. What was early gum made from?
2. Why do you think gum has been important to kids since colonial times?
3. Why do you think settlers added mint leaves to the spruce wax?
4. What do you think might be a problem with chewing gum made from trees?
5. Why might making the gum able to blow bubbles be important to kids?

7.

The tiny baby koala bear had just been born. The inch-long hairless baby immediately begins its journey up to its mother's pouch. Crawling through the fur, the blind baby miraculously finds its way to the pouch and crawls inside. There it stays cozy and well protected for the next seven months.

A furry foot or an ear might be the first sign that a baby koala is ready to leave its mother's pouch. After looking around and studying its environment, the baby will begin to leave the pouch during the days to a new perch on top of its mother's back. Its amazingly strong hands and feet keep the baby from falling off until it is ready to venture off alone.

1. How big did you visualize a koala when it is born?
2. Why do you think the koala heads straight to its mother's pouch?
3. Why do you think a baby koala has to stay in a pouch for so long?
4. Why do you think the baby moves out of its mother's pouch?
5. Why might the baby stay on its mother's back?

8.

Jesse Owens, a black man, was one of the greatest track and field athletes in history, but he was treated badly because of the color of his skin. He won four gold medals at the 1936 Olympic games in Germany. At the time, Germany's leader, Hitler, was claiming that only the people of his country would win medals. When Owens won, Hitler slipped out of the stadium to avoid having to shake his hand.

Jesse Owens was not bitter about the Olympics. When people wanted to know if he was angry, he reminded them that his own President hadn't invited him to the White House to shake hands, either. Jesse Owens proved himself above racism; he traveled the world as a goodwill ambassador for the U.S. Department of State. Later, he did much work at home to support youth organizations. In his speeches, Jesse Owens stressed that when the spirit of fair play learned in athletic competition is carried over into life, it helps people be kinder and more understanding to one another.

1. Where did Jesse Owens win his medals?
2. Why do you think Hitler tried to say Germans were the best?
3. What do you think Jesse Owens might have done as a "goodwill ambassador"?
4. What do you think Jesse Owens might have done to support youth organizations?
5. Do you think Jesse Owens became a hero to many people? Explain.

Level Eight

9.
two paragraphs

The crowd was silent as the young woman walked into the arena. Barely five feet tall and wearing her black hair in braids, Annie Oakley hardly looked old enough to be in the shooting contest. Frank Butler, a professional marksman, looked at the young woman and laughed. He was certain sure that his shooting title was not in jeopardy and that he would remain undefeated.

Frank picked up his rifle and quickly shot twenty-four of the twenty-five targets that were lined up. Annie congratulated Frank warmly. Then she lifted the rifle to her shoulder and rapidly fired at one target after another, hitting all twenty-five. Just fifteen years old, Annie would soon be on her way to international fame traveling the world as "Little Sure Shot" and Mrs. Frank Butler.

    1. How old was Annie Oakley when she won the shooting contest?
    2. Why might the crowd have been silent when Annie walked into the arena?
    3. Why do you think Frank Butler laughed when he saw her?
    4. Why do you think she became known as "Little Sure Shot"?
    5. What do you think it meant that she was known as Mrs. Frank Butler?

10.

Rosa Parks, a black woman, stepped on the bus and walked past the first five rows labeled "whites only." Although those seats were empty, Mrs. Parks moved to the middle section before she sat down exhausted from a long day at work. There she sat quietly watching the scenery of Montgomery, Alabama pass by as the driver made stop after stop.

Soon a white gentleman entered the bus and had no place to sit, so the driver turned and instructed all of the black people to move to the back of the bus. As instructed, each got up and stood in the back, except for Mrs. Parks. She was tired of being treated badly because of her skin color and refused to move. Realizing that she was not going to get up, the driver parked the bus and brought back a police officer who arrested Mrs. Parks. She did not struggle or argue as the officer calmly escorted her to jail.

Mrs. Parks was found guilty of disobeying the city's segregation laws and ordered to pay a fine, but again she refused. The black people of Montgomery supported Mrs. Parks and refused to ride the buses until the laws were changed. Almost one year later, after the Supreme Court ruled segregation to be illegal, Mrs. Parks rode the bus again. However, this time she rode in the front seat.

1. Where did Rosa Parks sit on the bus?
2. Why did the bus driver tell Mrs. Parks and the other black passengers to move to the back of the bus?
3. Why do you think Mrs. Parks did not struggle or argue when she was taken to jail?
4. Why do you think Mrs. Parks sat in the front seat the next time she got on a bus?
5. Explain why Rosa Parks is considered a heroine by many people?

Level Eight

11.

Ann Chen held her father's hand tightly as they went down the long narrow market street in Hong Kong. She could barely control her enthusiasm because today they would be shopping for something very special. Ann was mesmerized by the hundreds of ornate birdcages that lined the outside of the small shops. Inside each cage were colorful birds of every shape, color, and size, all expertly cared for by the merchants. Ann studied the cockatoos, parrots, and songbirds carefully as she tried to choose which one she would take home.

Halfway down the street, Ann stopped suddenly and pointed to a small shop where several silver and bamboo cages hung outside. Mr. Chen led his little daughter inside to a merchant who was using chopsticks to gently feed worms to his birds. The old man smiled at his tiny customer and then brought the cage down so Ann and her father could have a closer look at the bird she most desperately wanted.

Ann's eyes grew big with excitement as the merchant coaxed out a small songbird with beautiful black and yellow feathers. She stayed absolutely still when the man put the tiny bird on her shoulder and let it nibble gently on the tips of her short dark hair. Mr. Chen quickly paid the old man for Ann's songbird and a hand-made bamboo cage. Then the little girl, smiling from ear to ear, lovingly placed the little bird in the new birdcage. As she and her father began to walk down the street, a sweet melodious song could be heard coming from Ann's new pet. They were all happy to be going home.

    1. Where did you visualize Ann and her father shopping?
    2. Why do you think the merchant was feeding his birds with chopsticks?
    3. Why do you think Ann stayed still while the bird was on her shoulder?
    4. Why do you think the bird sang on the way home?
    5. What is a good title for this story?

12.

In 1953, Edmund Hillary, Tenzing Norgay, and 12 other climbers gathered at their base camp on Mt. Everest. Around them lay ropes, food, oxygen, and other supplies they would need for the climb up the highest peak in the world. They bundled themselves into layers of their warmest clothes and carefully packed the equipment. The climbers were all quiet for a moment as they looked up at the huge snow-covered mountain in the early morning light. Today they were going to begin their climb and try to be the first people to conquer the mountain.

The climbers slowly worked their way up the ice and rocks, often stopping to rest in the thin air. They had to set up several camps on the side of the massive peak where they could rest for several days before continuing up the slope. Approaching a large crevasse, Hillary sailed over it in a mighty jump. However, the ice on the other side gave way and Hillary began to fall into the deep hole. Luckily, he was tied to his partner Tenzing Norgay, who pulled Hillary to safety. The climbing could now continue.

After days struggling with the extreme cold and lack of oxygen, the climbers were ready for the final try at the top. Hillary and Norgay were chosen for the attempt. They ascended high into the clouds and slowly picked their way up a massive wall of ice before finally pulling themselves up to the top. As they looked around at the tremendous view, they saw there was nowhere higher that they could go. The world's tallest mountain had finally been conquered. Soon the names Hillary and Norgay would be famous around the world as the first to climb Mt. Everest.

1. How many people did you visualize on the team to climb Mt. Everest?
2. Why do you think the group carried oxygen with them to the top?
3. Why might the climbers need to wear layers of their warmest clothes?
4. What could have been a problem for Norgay being tied to Hillary?
5. What does it mean that "there was nowhere higher that they could go"?